Rhinoceroses

For Kids

Amazing Animal Books

For Young Readers

Mendon Cottage Books

JD-Biz Publishing

Read More Amazing Animal Books

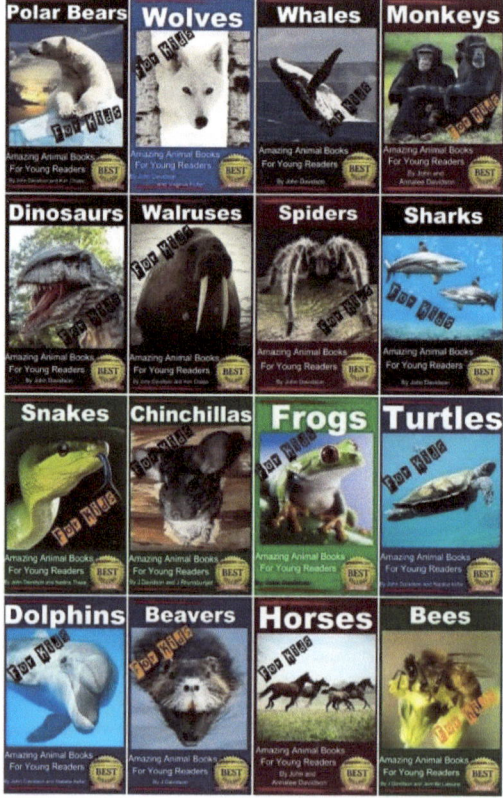

Download Free Books!

http://MendonCottageBooks.com

Table of Contents

Introduction

Rhinoceroses are one of the major attractions among all large land mammals in any zoo or a wildlife enclosure. This could be due to their heavily built body structure and horns that are unlike any other land mammal. Two species of Rhino live in Africa and three Rhino species live in Asia. The Asian rhinoceroses are quite smaller than their African counterparts.

These creatures, with their prehistoric looks, prefer the solitary life, which means they like to live by themselves. Sometimes you might see Rhinos charging trees or termite mounds. It is not because they are crazy, but more likely because of their weak eyesight. Surprising, isn't it? No wonder they rely on their sense of hearing, smell and of course their little friend, Oxpecker, who takes a free ride on them and alerts the Rhinos when they are danger, by sounding a special alarm.

Join us, as we explore the world of Rhinos including; their habitat, species, behavior, characteristics and some other interesting facts, while answering the most important question - Why are they faced with the risk of being critically endangered and who is really behind all of this? Are you curious? Then read on to find out. The answer might just surprise you.

About Rhinoceroses

Rhinoceroses are mammals that date back to Miocene era, which started about 23 million years ago. Out of the 5 species of rhinos alive today, two belong to Africa and the rest belong to Asia. The two African species are the Black rhinoceros and the White rhinoceros. The three Asian species are the Indian rhinoceros, Javan rhinoceros and the Sumatran rhinoceros. The two African species are among the 'Big 5' of the African safari. They contribute towards the economic development through the tourism industry which, in turn, creates job opportunities for the local communities.

A rhino's habitat can be the Savana Desert or a dense forest of subtropical and tropical regions. They are solitary creatures with both sexes having their territories established. Rhinoceroses are herbivores, meaning they eat plants and vegetation, with the White rhino being a grazer and others being browsers. The diet changes according to the availability of plant species depending on the seasons and rainfall. They have thick hides covering their body and can handle dry conditions better than many other species of animals living in that area.

Many valuable animals, as well as, plants are present in almost all conservation areas of rhinos. Therefore, they are also conserved while protecting rhinoceros. A rhinoceros's brain is relatively small in relation to their body size. They use their horns not only to battle for female rhinos and territories but also as self-defense against predators such as, tigers, lions and hyenas. Horns are a great help when breaking branches or digging up roots to gain access to food. The lifespan of a wild rhinoceros is 35 years but, it can live up to 40 years in captivity.

Characteristics

Rhinoceroses are easily recognizable due to their massive body, dermal horns and stumpy legs. Not all species of rhinos possess 2 horns. Some have just one which may be short or not visible at all. The skin color of a rhino is usually grey although individual shades depend on the soil conditions of the areas they graze and live for a certain extent of time. Their skin lacks hair almost entirely, but it is very thick and wrinkled. The skin around their shoulders could be around 1.5 inches in thickness. There is a one or two inch layer of fat just beneath their skin which helps them to maintain body temperature.

Rhinoceroses stand up to 6 feet tall and an adult typically weights from 1400 – 3600 Kg, which is equivalent to a small truck. Though males and females look similar in size, males are quite larger than females. Their feet have heavy hooves that help them walk through dense forests while crushing twigs and underbrush to leave a clear, broad trail behind them. Unlike Indricotherium, their ancient ancestor, which had a weight of 66,000 pounds, modern rhinoceroses look small.

Rhinoceroses are exclusive plant eaters. In other words they are herbivores. Browsers forage with their prehensile upper lips. This lip is more like a finger ideal for grasping twigs and branches. Unlike African species of rhinos, Asian rhino's incisors grow to be strong tusks. This helps these creatures to use them as weapons when fighting opponents. The male Indian rhinoceros's tusk can grow more than 3 inches in length, and is capable of slashing rivals with serious wounds.

Among all their other physical features, their horn is the most famous. It is interesting to note that the name 'rhinoceros' is derived from this very feature. In Greek terms, it means 'nose horn'. Although both African species of rhinoceros possess 2 horns each, only the Sumatran rhinos from the Asian species have two while the others have only one. These horns are made of keratin, not bone. They are used extensively in Asian folk medicine, although there are no scientific evidence to suggest that rhino horns have medicinal properties.

Behavior and Vocalization

Rhinoceroses often live in ranges that overlap with other territories of their kind. This leads to the sharing of resources such as water holes, feeding grounds, and wallows. Generally, the Black Rhino species is solitary, whiles the White rhino species are quite gregarious. Rhinoceroses have an ill temper which is aggravated more in areas where they are being disturbed constantly. Since their eyesight is poor, sometimes they are seen charging for no logical reason. However, their keen sense of hearing and smell makes up to their poor vision.

Rhinoceros has a wide vocabulary of snorts, grunts, squeaks, bellows and growls. In order to attack, they gallop with a speed of 30 mph after snorting with their heads lowered. Though they look clumsy, they are very agile creatures. Elephants and rhinos do not interact even though they share many of the same plants for food. Elephants can be really beneficial for digging wallows or pulling down branches of trees. Rhinos mark their territories using dung piles. They scrape their feet on their dung pile leaving a trail of scent which enables other members to identify them. It may be surprising, but rhinos have actually learned to be afraid of humans. They display defensive behaviors when a human scent is detected.

Rhinos show symbolic relationships with selected animal species. Cattle egrets sit on their back rarely picking on ectoparasites. The fork tailed drongo swoops down to feed on insects attracted to rhinos like flycatchers, but do not follow them away from home range. The red-billed oxpecker picks on insects present in a rhino's nostrils and ears while following them for a long distance. When danger is detected, these birds sound a high pitched call.

Rhinos can sleep both standing and lying on ground. They display a variety of visual signals as a means of communication apart from olfactory signals and vocalization. When curious or interested about something, they will straighten up their ears. If their ears go flat, that means they're angry and snorting is used when attacking.

Threats to Rhinoceros

Man is the main threat to any species of rhinoceros. In fact, adult rhinos do not have real predators in the wild, except for humans. They are creatures with a defined home range, and they go in search of waterholes where they are easily ambushed. Though they are large and tough, they're easily poached by humans. Poaching became an increased global threat in December 2009, and efforts to save the rhinos became ineffective. So, what is the real reason to hunt such animals? The answer lies right on their face. Yes, the rhino horn. That's what people are after. Popular beliefs such as rhino horns having the ability to heal typhoid, fevers, jaundice, headaches, and vomiting has prompted poachers to go after these animals. Spiritual beliefs to evade evil and creations of artistic work have prompted the killing of rhinos at an alarming rate.

Sumatran rhinoceros and the Javan rhinoceros, two species from Asia, are critically endangered. In 2010, when the Javan rhinoceros faced extinction in Vietnam, only a very few were found in Indonesia and Java. The Black rhinoceros is also critically endangered. However, due to some conservation efforts, they are now increasing in number and are found to be living in nine countries of Africa.

Although the Southern White rhinoceros is estimated to be around 20,000, the Northern white rhinoceros is critically endangered. Rhinoceros horns fetch a large amount of money from the black market, and this is one of the major reasons to poach these creatures.

Asia, especially Vietnam, is considered to be the largest market for horns of rhinoceroses. The rhino horn is made of keratin, the same substance found in hair and fingernails. If people believed that ground powder from hair and nails can heal the illnesses which they seem to think that a rhino horn could, we might be able to spare the life of some rhinos out in the wild.

White Rhinoceros

White rhinoceros is also known as the Square lipped rhinoceros. They live in the grassy plains of Africa, as they prefer grasslands and savannah as their habitat. They have a square shaped lip which perfectly suits their diet, as they are among the largest pure grazers. They graze on grass and short grains while walking and lowering their enormous heads and lips to the ground. They drink water twice a day but if the conditions are dry they can go up to 3 or 4 days with no water. White rhinos are the biggest among all five species of rhinos. The males are quite heavier than the females. The largest white rhinoceros ever to be recorded had a weight of 4,500 Kg. They are the 4th largest land mammal in the world after three different species of elephants, and are the most abundant species among all rhinos.

White rhinoceroses have a large head supported by a massive body with a short neck. The length of the male body including the head is around 3.7 to 4 m, while it is slightly less in females. There are 2 horn-like growths on its snout close to each other. The horn present at the front is larger and it grows up to 90cm on average. These horns differ in shape and composition when compared to other animals having horns such as cattle and deer. Horns of rhinoceroses are made of solid keratin. Three toes are present in each foot. White rhinoceros have a hump behind its neck which is quite visible. They have ears which move independently in order to pick up sound, however they depend mostly on their sense of smell. This explains why they possess olfactory passages larger than their whole brain. Two subspecies of white rhinoceros are the northern white rhinoceros and the southern white rhinoceros, with the former being rarer than the latter. Some may wonder whether White rhinos are really white in color, but it is not so. They are actually grey in color and are the most social among all species of rhinos.

Most adult male white rhinoceroses are solitary while females live in herds of 14 most often. Dominant bulls use urine and excrement to mark their territories. These rhinos love wallowing in mud holes coating their skin with a natural sunscreen and a bug repellent. They also have the habit of taking cover from the harsh sun by lying in shady areas. They make use of sounds to communicate in different situations. Growls, squeals, grunts and snorts are some such examples. An interesting thing about these creatures is that they can run up to 50 km/hr.

Black Rhinoceros

Black rhinoceros is also known as the hook-lipped rhinoceros. They are native to central and eastern Africa including; South Africa, Zimbabwe, Kenya, Cameroon, Angola, Tanzania and Namibia. White rhinos are not white in color and similarly Black rhinos are not black in color. In fact, they are either brown or grey. They can be easily distinguished from a White rhinoceros by their size and small ears. Their head is positioned higher than a

White rhinoceros because they are browsers unlike a White rhino which is a grazer. The prehensile upper lip which appears to be hooked, is used in grasping twigs or leaves when feeding.

Typically an adult Black rhinoceros weights from 800 to 1400 kg, though there have been reports of males weighing well over 1500 Kg. Females are slightly smaller than males. An adult stands up to 132 – 180cm at shoulder level. The presence of 2 horns helps them to break branches, dig up roots or use as a self-defense to intimidate predators. Sometimes, the growth of a small third horn is visible. Black rhinos have a thick layered skin which protects them from sharp grasses and thorns. It is also a dwelling place for external parasites such as ticks and mites which are eaten by egrets and oxpeckers. Though this behavior was thought to be on mutualism, recent studies suggest that oxpeckers could be parasites feeding on blood.

Due to the presence of poor eyesight, Black rhinoceroses rely heavily on their sense of hearing and smell. Their ears could be rotated independently to the direction of sound. They also have the ability to hear from a very vast distance away. Their keen sense of smell allows them to detect predators. A Black rhinoceros's territory often overlaps with another rhino's territory. Their home range depends mainly on the season and the availability of food resources. The size and the nature of each range depend mainly on the individual's age and gender, while females prefer large ranges when having calves.

Black rhinoceroses are known to be extremely aggressive, with a tendency to charge at anything perceived as a threat to them. They do not hesitate to fight with each other. Around 30% of females and 50% of males die of injuries related to combats.

Indian Rhinoceros

Indian rhinoceros are also known as the Indian one-horned rhinoceros and the greater one horned rhinoceros. They are found in Assam of north eastern India and protected areas of Terai in Nepal. The Indian rhinoceros is the 2nd largest among all the other rhino species. Though they are the 5th largest land animal, they are placed 2nd among native land mammals of Asia. The average head and body length of a male is 368 -380cm while it is slightly less in females. They have a heavy skull with body hair present only on ear fringes, tail brush and eyelashes. They have silver brown skin which is thick but appears pinkish near large skin folds covering the body. Wart-like bumps are present on its shoulders and upper legs. Males have neck folds which are thick.

The Indian rhinoceroses were abundant once throughout the Indo-gangetic Plain, but its natural habitat was reduced drastically because of excessive hunting. At present, only 3,000 of this species live in the wild, out of which India's Assam is home to 2,000 of them. Though these creatures congregate around bathing areas, they are actually solitary animals. Their home ranges overlap with one another as dominant males do not mind other males passing through their territory, except during the breeding season. Indian rhinos are active both early in the morning and night. They are great swimmers as well as runners having the ability to reach running speeds up to 55 km/hr for a short period of time.

The diet of an Indian rhinoceros is primarily made of grasses, though they also consume fruits, leaves, branches of trees and shrubs apart from floating or submerged aquatic plants. In order to communicate, they are known to use distinct vocalizations such as roaring, shrieking, honking, moo-grunting, rumbling, snorting, thumping, squeak-panting, bleating and groaning apart from olfactory communication. They spend their midday wallowing in rivers, puddles, lakes and ponds in order to cool themselves.

Javan Rhinoceros

http://www.asianrhinos.org.au/index.php/species/javan_rhinoceros/

The Javan rhinoceros is also known as the lesser one-horned rhinoceros or the Sunda rhinoceros. They are one of the largest animals in Indonesia second only to the Asian elephants but are the largest in Java. Similar to an Indian rhinoceros, this species have only a single horn which is the smallest among all rhino species with its length generally less than 7.9 inches. However, it is interesting to note that only males have horns and not females. Though these rhinos do not tend to use their horns to fight others, they are most certainly used to clear paths through dense vegetation, bring down plants for eating, and scrape mud in wallows. This rhino has an armored appearance due to the natural mosaic pattern present on its skin. The neck folds, resembling saddles, present over the shoulder, are quite smaller than those found in an Indian rhinoceros.

Javan rhinoceroses prefer using wallows of other animals or natural pits without digging their own wallows. They make use of their horns to enlarge such wallows. Wallowing does not only help cool the body but it also helps in preventing parasitic infections and diseases. Small groups congregate near salt licks other than mud wallows. Salt licks provide essential nutrients to rhinos. Home ranges of males are larger than females. Territorial overlapping is present. However, the prevalence of territorial fights is not known. Males use dung piles and urine to mark their territories. Other species of rhinos have an unusual habit of scraping their back feet in their dung pile after defecating. However, the Javan rhinos do not do so even though they defecate in piles. This change in behavior is thought to have occurred due to the difference in ecology as Javan and Sumatran wet forests may not require spreading of odors with such methods.

Javan rhinoceroses are herbivorous animals that consume a variety of plant species including twigs, shoots, fallen fruits and young foliage. They are the most adaptable feeders among all species of rhinos. This species is less vocal than the Sumatran rhinoceros. In areas like Vietnam, these creatures are known to retreat into thick forests when humans are close by.

Sumatran Rhinoceros

The Sumatran rhinoceros is the smallest rhinoceros among all the other species of rhinoceros. They stand from 112 to 145cm at shoulder level and their body length is around 250cm. They usually weigh from 500 to 1000 kg on average and possess 2 horns just like the Black and White rhinoceros. The nasal horn is the largest among the two, also known as the anterior horn, while the other is more like a stub known as the frontal horn. Horns are either black or dark grey in color. Male rhinos have bigger horns than females. Sumatran rhinoceros lives in cloud forests, swamps, highland and lowland secondary rainforest. They inhabit areas that are hilly and close to water, especially steep upper valleys accompanied by copious undergrowth. Males usually have a larger home range than the females. However, their ranges overlap with one another, whereas, territorial overlapping is not seen among the ranges of females as they are spaced apart. Marking of territory is done by leaving excrement, scraping soil using their feet or bending saplings to form distinct patterns. However there is no evidence to suggest that Sumatran rhinos fight to defend their territories.

Sumatran rhinos are active mostly at dawn, just after dusk, or when eating. They move to lower areas within their range when the months get cooler, but they move to higher areas during the rainy season. The rhinos will deepen puddles using their horns and feet, if mud holes become unavailable. Captive bred species have seemed to have developed eye problems, inflamed skins, nails, hair loss, and suppurations, and have died eventually due to the deprivation of adequate wallowing. Sumatran rhinoceroses are browsers like the Black rhinoceros and their diet consists of leaves, shoots, twigs, fruits and young saplings. Generally, up to 50kg of food is consumed by a rhino each day. Though their horns are very much smaller than those of the African species, they are being poached for their horns and valued at a very high price. This is the reason why the population of this species has declined at an alarming rate over the past centuries. The lifespan of a Sumatran rhinoceros in the wild is estimated to be around 30-45 years.

Interesting facts about the Rhinoceros

Several other species of animals having a horn-like appendage over their nose has a 'rhinoceros' in front of their name. For example, rhinoceros fish, rhinoceros beetle, rhinoceros rat snake, rhinoceros cockroach, rhinoceros iguana, rhinoceros chameleon, rhinoceros viper, and rhinoceros hornbill all get their names from having a horn-like appendage. Zoologists grouped elephants, pigs, horses, tapirs and rhinos as pachyderms many years ago, due to the presence of thick skin. Pachyderm is a Greek term which means 'thick skin'. Even today, this name is used occasionally.

Many famous people such as the guitarist Larry Reinhardt, former British soccer player David Unsworth, and professional American wrestler and actor

Terry Gerin are nicknamed as 'Rhino'. Even the national rugby teams of Indonesia and South Africa are known as Rhinos. A rhino's horn continues to grow throughout its lifetime. The longest ever recorded horn belonged to a white rhino and it measured just below 5 feet. Animals such as horses, Zebras, and tapirs are known as odd toed ungulates and are the closest living relatives of rhinos. A group of bees is called a Swarm. Similarly a group of fish is called a school. But what do you call a group of rhinos? It's called a crash or herd.

A female rhino's dung smells different from a male rhino's dung. There is a difference of smell in a young rhino's dung and an adult rhino's dung, which makes the dung an indicator to identify a particular individual. Communal or multiple dung deposits are called middens. Though humans are the number one predators of rhinoceros, two other animals are reported to have preyed upon rhinos, especially young ones. They are the tigers of Asia and the lions of Africa. However, wild dogs, hyenas, Nile crocodiles and leopards have also killed rhino calves in Africa occasionally.

The 1st Sumatran Rhinoceros to be born in captivity after a century was named as 'Andatu'. He was born in the Sumatran Rhino Sanctuary weighing 60 pounds in the year 2012. In Indonesian language, Andatu means 'A Gift from God'.

Similar to World Aids Day and World Environment Day, there is a day dedicated especially for Rhinos. It is called the World Rhino day and is celebrated on the 22nd of September each year.

Rhinoceros in different cultures

Rhinoceros had been depicted in popular culture mainly because of their enormous size. The earliest wood carving of a rhinoceros dating back to 1515 was found. Since it was not very accurate, it could be assumed that the artist had a very hard time carving it on the wood or he had not seen a real rhino. Either way, it shows that humans had an interest towards rhinoceros from the beginning.

Malaysians had a special place for rhinoceroses in their culture. Written materials bear witness to such ideas. A legend states that rhinoceros used to put out fire in forests in order to protect the habitats of other animals. Some stories even suggest that they used to come to the villages to stop the fire from destroying people and their belongings. It could be said that rhinos were portrayed positively in Malaysian culture. Ground up horns of rhinoceroses had been used in the making of Chinese medicine for hundreds of years which is even continued today. This practice has put these creatures into a high risk of extinction. In Asia, the rhino horns are used for medicine or other creations such as decorative art work. In countries like Yemen, handles of weapons, such as daggers, were made using horns. Though selling of such weapons is considered illegal, they are sold in the black market for very high prices.

Rhinoceros is used as a mascot for many logos by advertisers. They believe it portrays the correct image of being tough and strong. The Rhino Lining is one such example. In Swazi culture, plants and animals, including the rhinos, are given human attributes so that the listener will be able to identify the characteristics that exist within their inner self. This makes the moral of a story much easier to convey in an effective manner. In China, the form of rhinoceros is used in making beautiful pieces of art. The discovery of the bronze Zun wine vessel in 1843 confirms the above fact.

Rhinos are also used in TV programs and movies such as 'The Gods Must be Crazy' and 'Ace Ventura Pet Detective.'

Join our newsletter and receive

Top Ten **Dog Breeds** For Kids

Amazing Animal Books For Young Readers
Kisha Bennett & John Davidson

German Shepherds

Dog Books for Kids
K. Bennett

Bulldogs

Dog Books for Kids
K. Bennett

Dachshund

Dog Books for Kids
K. Bennett

Poodles

Dog Books for Kids
K. Bennett

Labrador Retrievers

Dog Books for Kids
K. Bennett

Rottweilers

Dog Books for Kids
K. Bennett

Boxers

Dog Books for Kids
K. Bennett

Golden Retrievers

Dog Books for Kids
K. Bennett

Puppies

Dog Books For Kids

AmazingAnimalBooks
By John Davidson

Beagles

Dog Books for Kids
K. Bennett

Yorkshire Terriers

Dog Books for Kids
K. Bennett

Dogs

Top Ten Dog Breeds For Kids

Amazing Animal Books For Young Readers
Zahra Jazeel & John Davidson

Cats For Kids

Amazing Animal Books For Young Readers
K. Bennett & John Davidson

Foxes For Kids

Amazing Animal Books For Young Readers
Zahra Jazeel & John Davidson

Wolves For Kids

Amazing Animal Books For Young Readers
By John Davidson and Virginia Fidler

Our books are available at

1. Amazon.com

2. Barnes and Noble

3. Itunes

4. Kobo

5. Smashwords

6. Google Play Books

Download Free Books!

http://MendonCottageBooks.com

Publisher

JD-Biz Corp

P O Box 374

Mendon, Utah 84325

http://www.jd-biz.com/

Mendon Cottage Books

P O Box 374, Mendon Utah 84325

www.ingramcontent.com/pod-product-compliance
Lightning Source LLC
Chambersburg PA
CBHW050909290526
45792CB00002B/750